MW00700953

Every

of the

Step

Way

Britney: Every Step of the Way

ONYX
Published by New American Library, a division of
Penguin Putnam Inc., 375 Hudson Street,
New York, New York 10014, U.S.A.
Penguin Books Ltd, 27 Wrights Lane,
London W8 5TZ, England
Penguin Books Australia Ltd, Ringwood,
Victoria, Australia
Penguin Books Canada Ltd, 10 Alcorn Avenue,
Toronto, Ontario, Canada M4V 3B2
Penguin Books (N.Z.) Ltd, 182–190 Wairau Road,
Auckland 10, New Zealand

Penguin Books Ltd, Registered Offices:
Harmondsworth, Middlesex, England

First published by Onyx, an imprint of New American Library,
a division of Penguin Putnam Inc.

First Printing, August 2000
10 9 8 7 6 5 4 3 2 1

Copyright © Felicia Culotta, 2000
All rights reserved

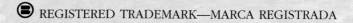 REGISTERED TRADEMARK—MARCA REGISTRADA

Printed in the United States of America

Without limiting the rights under copyright reserved above, no part of this publication may be reproduced, stored in or introduced into a retrieval system, or transmitted, in any form, or by any means (electronic, mechanical, photocopying, recording, or otherwise), without the prior written permission of both the copyright owner and the above publisher of this book.

BOOKS ARE AVAILABLE AT QUANTITY DISCOUNTS WHEN USED TO PROMOTE PRODUCTS OR SERVICES. FOR INFORMATION PLEASE WRITE TO PREMIUM MARKETING DIVISION, PENGUIN PUTNAM INC., 375 HUDSON STREET, NEW YORK, NEW YORK 10014.

Dedication

My photo journal is dedicated to all the smiling faces in this book—those we met and those whose lives were touched in any way by my sweet friend Britney Spears!

❤ ❤ ❤ ❤ ❤ ❤ ❤ ❤ ❤ ❤ ❤ ❤

Acknowledgments

To Lynne Spears, who was the first to tell me my pictures were book-worthy

To my dad, Vince, and my sister, Vicki, for the gift of the camera with which to capture the world (and Britney) on all our travels

To Kim Kaiman and Danielle Butin for knowing just the right kind of folks (primarily Carolyn Nichols, the Executive Director, Editorial, at New American Library, and Karen Gantz-Zahler, lawyer and literary agent)

To my sweet friends for their tons of encouragement—Jill, Debbie, Amy, Carol, Rachel, Judi, Noni, Angie, Sarah, Sonia, Jane, J.T., Anthony, Tammi, Carol Anne, Todd and Tracy, Hayley, Theresa, Rob, Q, Johnny, Aaron, Carlos, Marilyn Max and Crew, (E.K. & O!), Beatrice, Betty, Sean, Michele, Lisa, Leigh, Paul, Marijo, Kim, Jackie, Richard, Jerry, Don, Joy …

and last, but not least, to Brit. Without her loyalty and friendship there never would have been a single goofy—or gorgeous!—pose!

SPRING 2000

Hello from Britney

When I'm being interviewed, I'm often asked about my grueling work schedule that leaves me little time to do much else. How do I keep my energy going show after show? What grounds me, making me stay confident—and sane—when the whole world is watching every step I take? In a word, the answer to all these questions is *Felicia*. Since 1997, when I left my hometown to make *Baby One More Time*, Felicia has been at my side. She makes sure I'm comfortable wherever I go. She's so normal, so down-to-earth. We laugh a lot together. Sometimes we cry.

It gets kind of lonely when I'm on the road. I can't go outside the hotel room without causing a riot. I love what I do, but occasionally I miss my old life. When I miss my mom and the advice she gives me, Felicia comes through. She is really like a big sister. She keeps me humble because she's not afraid to tell me the truth. She believes in my dreams.

God has given me many gifts—talent, determination, family and friends, and tremendous good fortune. He's also given me Felicia, who's always there, armed with a notebook and a camera. I hope you enjoy her pictures.

SPRING 2000

Hello from Felicia

Ten years ago I was working as a pediatric dental hygienist near Kentwood, Louisiana, when I met Lynne Spears. She told me all about her daughter, who was eight at the time, and invited me to watch little Britney perform at a local crafts fair. This girl with brown curls walked confidently across the makeshift stage and began to sing—in this incredibly strong, amazingly mature voice. Britney entertained the crowd, then came off the stage, took my hand, and asked, "Will you help me go pick out a new baby doll?"

After that I moved away from the South to work as a nanny—I'm pretty good with kids—and Brit went on to her training and performing, doing the *Mickey Mouse Club* and live theater. In September 1997, the day after I quit my nanny job, I got a call from Lynne Spears. Britney, now fifteen, had just signed a deal with Jive Records and had to go to New York. Lynne couldn't go because she was needed at home with Brit's five-year-old sister Jamie Lynn. Would I be able to work as Britney's personal assistant for a few months?

Personal assistant? What did that mean? Neither one of us was exactly sure. I would keep Britney's daily schedule—make sure she showed up on time to rehearsals and promotional appearances—and stay with her twenty-four hours a day as a kind of surrogate big sister. It sounded pretty easy. I thought, three months I'll work with her— that's it. After all, how many teenage singers really become big stars? But never for even a second in my heart did I think she wouldn't make it. Sometimes you just feel it, you just know.

Needless to say, neither Britney nor I was quite prepared for what happened next. Almost immediately after the album *Baby One More Time* was released, Britney soared up the pop charts. Since then she has been in constant demand for concerts and appearances. Everyone wants to take her picture or talk to her. She's mobbed anyplace she goes. So much for easy, right?

The last three years have been incredible—for both of us. I have a really neat life! I've met hundreds of people, stayed in countless hotel suites, traveled around the globe, and even starred in a music video. But helping Britney to reach for her dreams has been the most fulfilling experience of my life. Most people see Britney as a glossy celebrity. Sometimes it makes me sad that they don't remember that she's a human being with feelings that get bruised by hurtful remarks. I hope that here you will glimpse the special and tender-hearted girl she really is.

I've watched from behind the scenes as Brit has grown up in front of the world. Along the way I've tried to capture the fun of our great adventure on film, as a personal scrapbook. My collection of photos grew enormous, and now I'm running out of places to put them. I wasn't sure if anyone would ever want to look at them besides maybe Brit's family and myself, because they're not professional-quality shots. But then I realized they tell a unique and wonderful story. So, here's *my* Britney Spears album.

Felicia

My first day on the job as Britney's personal assistant.
I look more nervous than she does!

Girls' night out

In **September 1997**, **Brit** and I went to dinner alone in **New Orleans** to get to know each other before heading off to **New York**. I had no idea what was in store for me, but we were both determined to have fun.

Britney got one last hug from **Mom** at the **Louisiana** airport. It was very difficult for **Lynne Spears** to send fifteen-year-old **Britney** off. But her daughter had worked so hard to secure the record deal with **Jive**, **Lynne** knew **Brit** was ready to fly!

Britney was in the recording studio every day. Here she was working on lyrics with "Bo Legged" Lou. When's the lunch break?

Music in Full Force
Britney on the keyboard at Full Force Studios in late 1997.

Here Brit was practicing a couple of the songs she would record for *Baby One More Time.*

The Cheiron recording studio in Stockholm, Sweden, where Brit recorded *Baby One More Time.*

Britney with songwriter Max Martin. On the computer screen in front of them were the lyrics for the single ". . . Baby One More Time." Max has worked for a number of young pop groups—including the Backstreet Boys—as both a producer and writer. He also wrote "I'll Be There" and "Crazy" for Britney.

Brit took an impromptu guitar lesson with producer Eric Foster White in his New Jersey studio. He's worked with Whitney Houston, one of Britney's favorite artists. Eric wrote, among others, "Soda Pop" and "From the Bottom of My Broken Heart."

A game of darts with Eric after a long day in the recording studio.

Back in New York, Brit prepares for her first photo shoot.

Here it's time for hair and makeup. For some unknown reason, her hair turned orange. She was so upset until the hairdresser fixed it just right.

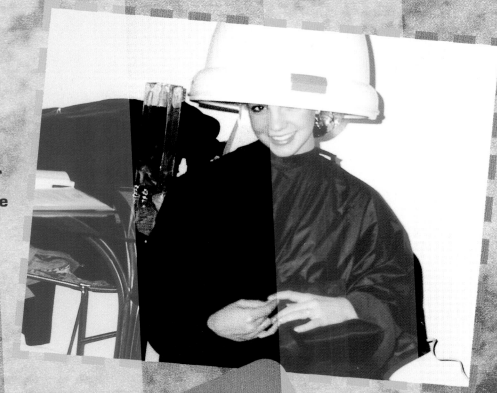

**The end result.
Ready to get off the phone and pose.**

The Big Apple! Jive Records put us in an apartment with this spectacular view of the New York skyline.

In the New York apartment singing along with her rehearsal tape. Hmm . . . chips!

In Nashville, during spring 1998, Britney was featured at her very first Jive/BMG showcase. She had to get up and sing a few songs in front of the corporate executives. We bought this dress for $70.00 at XOXO. She was ready to "wow!" them. And did!

Jive sent Britney out on a summer 1998 "mall tour" sponsored by *Teen* and *Seventeen* magazines. She and the dancers performed numbers that later appeared on the *BOMT* album, among others, "Soda Pop" and "From the Bottom of My Broken Heart."

These two cute guys from "Saved by the Bell"—Anthony Harrell and Tom Huntington—acted as MCs for the tour.

After the malls we visited radio stations to beg them to play the ". . . Baby One More Time" single. We had to do some crazy things to get Britney's name out there. That's Jack Satter from Jive on the left and *me* on the steer. (Brit was too scared to get on.)

At least I didn't have to ride on top of the van. Denise George from Jive posed with us.

One more promo.
Please play Brit's song!

The single ". . . Baby One More Time" was released in October 1998. Concert dates were piling up. There was one thing left to do—go film the video! Here we are after a very early arrival in Los Angeles the day of the shoot.

Taking a break during dance rehearsal are choreographer Randy Conner and two of the back-up dancers who worked on the video.

Watching from the sidelines, Britney and *BOMT* director Nigel Dick, who also worked on the Backstreet Boys' "As Long As You Love Me" and Cher's "Believe" videos.

Britney (in curlers) with her cousin Chad, who played her "love interest" in the video. We picked him because at the time we didn't know that many guys and Chad was working as a model for Abercrombie and Fitch. He's very photogenic. Must run in Brit's family!

The outfit!

Wardrobe maven Stephanie and an assistant made some final adjustments to Brit's notorious "school girl uniform." Brit raised eyebrows when she chose this costume herself.

Brit, two dancers—Marlene and Yxia—and me (in schoolmarm glasses) posed between takes.

Brit and me ready to "rock 'n' roll." The video was filmed at Rydell High of *Grease* fame, which is actually Venice Beach High School.

In November 1998, Brit left on a three-month tour as the opening act for 'N Sync. Here's our beloved tour bus—home sweet home on the road—from Florida Coach.

The bus gang. The crew included four dancers—Tania Ante, TJ Espinosa, Jeri Slaughter, and Charissa Seaman—tour manager David Green, hair/makeup expert Tina Lamertina, driver J. T. Kline, the star in the middle, and her personal assistant, me, on the left.

Britney and the dancers —
Tania, TJ, Jeri, and Charissa — before the show.

I posed with the group after a costume change backstage.

A " good luck "
hug before the
first show

Britney celebrated her seventeenth birthday on tour December 2, 1998 — the same day her single ". . . Baby One More Time" went gold, selling 500,000 copies in one day!

Brit and Tania peeking out from behind the balloons.

What's more fun than a silly string fight?

3'98

. . . Having 'N Sync sing you "Happy Birthday!"

Since their early days with the
Mickey Mouse Club, 'N Sync's JC Chasez and Justin
Timberlake have remained buds with Brit.

Crazy bus games.

The silly guy in the bear ears leaning against Brit is Steven,
the brother of 'N Sync's Joey Fatone.

A bus party with 'N Sync and our crew between cities.

Justin, Brit and Lance raided Britney's wig trunk.

*Fact: Brit's favorite U.S. city is Chicago, where she can shop at her favorite store: Sugar Magnolia.

Two Southern pals
Lance and Brit in a less silly moment.

The "Born to Make You Happy" video, take one. It was directed by **Billy Woodruff**, who made **"I'll Never Break Your Heart"** with the **Backstreet Boys.**

*Fact: This video was made for international release only. You can see it in the U.S. if you go to ane of Brit's concerts!

Britney really shines; her costume perfectly matched the set.

Brit and seventeen-year-old choreographer Wade Robson, who worked on the Grammys and MTV Europe.

Britney posed in one of her "Born" costumes.

The crew took a break to watch the video playback.

Another background, another outfit. Brit all in white.

*Fact: Wade Robeson was Michael Jackson's protégé. He came to Michael's attention after winning a dance contest in his native Australia. He's still best friend with the "gloved one."

**Christopher Snyder played Brit's
"love interest" in "Born to Make You Happy."
He's so cute. . . and tall!**

The "From the Bottom of My Broken Heart" video was filmed in a Los Angeles suburb. Here Britney's waiting for the bus — and the cameras to roll.

Brit with "love interest" Christopher Snyder — again!

Building the success of *BOMT* meant lots of world travel. Britney and I got to see so many gorgeous places. Here we were in the German Alps, where Brit filmed a Disney special.

The first time these two Southern girls have ever played in deep snow

While on tour, Britney is usually too tired to get out and sightsee, but this trip gave her time to relax a little.

Brit struck a pose in a kimono for a Japanese teen magazine.

Brit in Japan to promote the ". . . Baby One More Time" single. Here she's playing a video game with Michael Galbe — Jive's international rep.

Brit bought this hat and glasses on the street in Tokyo.

She thought she looked so cool!

Brit surrounded by fans during a Canadian interview in 1998. She was huge in Canada before hitting the charts in the U.S.

A gelato (ice cream) break in Rome, summer 1999.

Madrid!

Spring 1999

Monaco!

**May 1999 for the World Music Awards.
I loved the Riviera. I think it's the most intriguing place
we've visited so far. Brit prefers Paris.**

*Fact:
In Monaco,
Brit and I lay
by the pool near
Ricky Martin.
Heaven!*

***Fact: Brit was thrilled when Cher stopped
to thank her for the great job she did singing
"And the Beat Goes On" during the Cher tribute.**

Who's that lady? Onstage and off, Britney has a great time posing. Here she was in her Cher wig for her performance of "And the Beat Goes On" at the World Music Awards.

Brit's all ready for a *long* overseas flight.

Goin' country on the tour bus in driver J.T.'s hat.

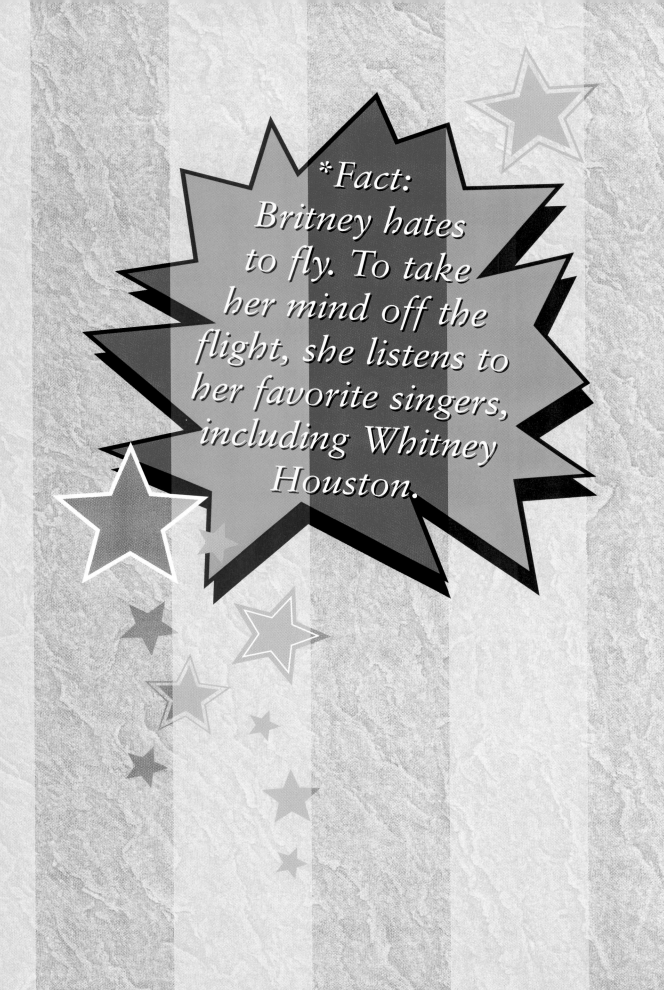

Britney before a show in Atlanta, GA —
one stop on the *BOMT* tour.
Check out her dressing room rider
(supplies) — water, fruit, Pop-Tarts,
and cereal to snack on.

In Hershey, PA, Brit
rocked out on air guitar
before a concert.
(The guitar is plastic; she
won it in the amusement
park during the trip.)

The Spears family before Britney's first concert of the *BOMT* tour. From left: Lynne, Jamie, Britney, Bryan, and girlfriend Blaize.

The Spear sisters.
Brit gave Jamie Lynn a hug while dancer Charissa looks on.

The Spears family portrait at the
Teen Choice Awards in summer 1999.
From left: Jamie, Lynne, Britney, Jamie Lynn
and Bryan.

Credit: Arnold Turner

Credit: Arnold Turner.

Britney and 98° at Teen Choice Awards, summer 1999 in Los Angeles

Brit sometimes gets nervous meeting people, especially other entertainers whose work she admires. At MTV Europe in Dublin, she posed with the fabulous Whitney Houston, November 1999.

American Woman Brit was overwhelmed when she met rocker Lenny Kravitz. He spent the day with us and his friend Mark Selliger at Brit's *Oops* album cover shoot.

Another great singer,
Mariah Carey, also
appeared at MTV Europe.

During the 'N Sync tour, Brit met the Olsen twins — sister Jamie Lynn's favorites.

Britney and I speak with Angelica Pickles at *The Rugrats Movie* premiere. We're using bowling bags as purses!

Meet the Moffats! Brit did at the Much Music Awards in Toronto, 1999.

Jamiroquai's Jason Kay and Brit shared smiles at MTV Europe, Dublin, November 1999.

Brit fit right in with the other blondes
in the smash country group, the Dixie Chicks,
before the Grammy Awards, March 2000.
The group took home an award for
Best Country Album.

**Brit met Babyface at
Teen People's third anniversary
party in Los Angeles,
January 2000.**

*Fact:
Both LFO
and Bosson
opened for
Britney during
her "Crazy"
tour.

With LFO at the *Teen People* party.

"One in a Million" Swedish singing
sensation Bosson with Britney.

**Brit with Enrique Iglesias
and assistant stylist Claudette.
Brit is one of Enrique's biggest fans.**

**Brit with teen skating sensation
and Olympic medallist Tara Lipinski.
She's a real fan and has sat in the VIP section
at Britney's concerts.**

In December 1999, Britney was asked to perform at the annual tree lighting ceremony in Rockefeller Center, New York City. Here she was with *The Today Show*'s Matt Lauer, who hosted the event.

Yuletide carols being sung by 'N Sync. . . .
Happy holidays from Brit and the boys.

Hair!

The "Crazy" video was filmed at a power plant and starred Melissa
Joan Hart of *Sabrina the Teenage Witch*. Here Britney and her
manager, Larry Rudolph, scope out the location. We all had to wear
hard hats.

A break from shooting. From left: Charissa, me,
Britney, Melissa Joan Hart, and Tania.

"Crazy" was featured on the soundtrack for the movie *Drive Me Crazy,* starring Melissa Joan Hart. Here she and Brit visited MTV to promote it.

Brit and Melissa performed a makeover on this lucky guy for an MTV spot. (This is "after.")

A little downtime on a hotel room couch.
Brit gets so tired from the nonstop touring that she
grabs a catnap wherever she can.

We're platinum! Brit and company celebrate
the *BOMT* album's success. From left: Larry Rudolph,
Brit's lawyer/manager; Barry Weiss, president
of Jive; and Johnny Wright, manager extraordinaire.
To date, *BOMT* has sold 20 million copies worldwide.

Britney loves clothes. Here she's choosing a costume for one of her video shoots.

*Fact: Hayley Hill designed the costumes for two of Brit's tours.

Brit leaving for *Teen People*'s third anniversary party with fashion editor Hayley Hill.

Britney on the way to the 1999 MTV Awards, where she was up for Best Female Video. I relived my "teacher" role from the ". . . Baby One More Time" video on stage during Brit's dance number with 'N Sync.

Britney ready to perform at the Billboard Awards. For the number, Brit had to emerge from a time capsule of smoky dry ice. The fringe from her costume kept getting stuck, so I had to crouch under the smoke throughout her entire performance in a 2' x 2' box to make sure the strings didn't tangle.

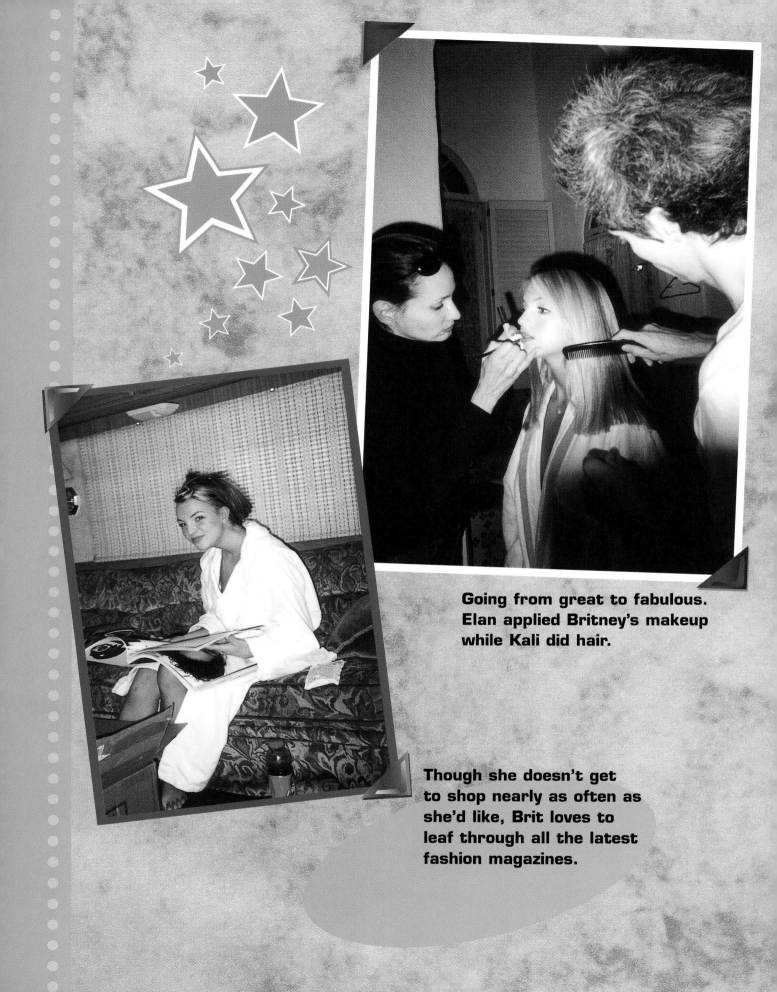

Going from great to fabulous. Elan applied Britney's makeup while Kali did hair.

Though she doesn't get to shop nearly as often as she'd like, Brit loves to leaf through all the latest fashion magazines.

Dressed for the Billboard Music Awards, Las Vegas, December 1999. She was nominated for and won four awards that night.

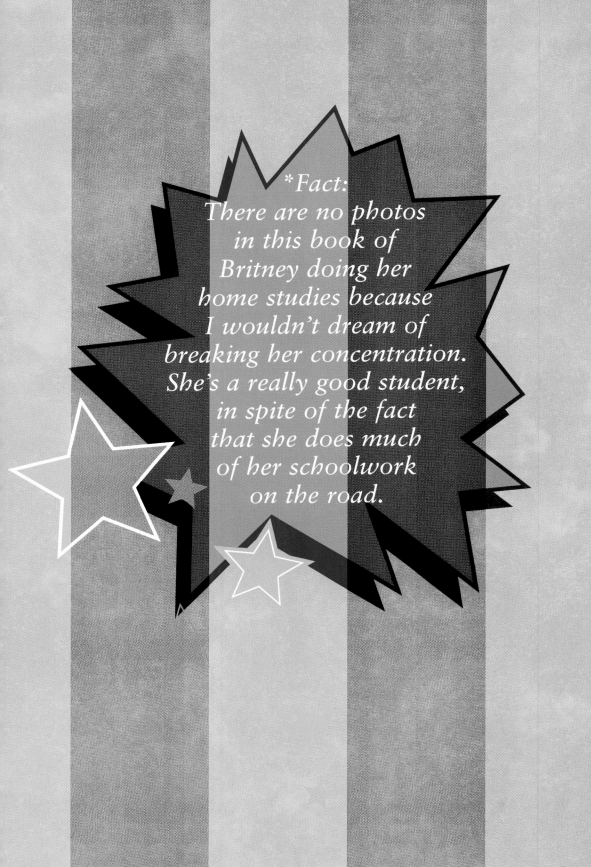

*Fact:
There are no photos
in this book of
Britney doing her
home studies because
I wouldn't dream of
breaking her concentration.
She's a really good student,
in spite of the fact
that she does much
of her schoolwork
on the road.

In November 1999, Britney returned to Cheiron to record her next album. Here Brit climbed the stairway to success inside the studio.

Brit with Steve Lunt of Jive and Max Martin (nice haircut!), hoping to make magic one more time. In fact, Max wrote the title track for the album, "Oops. . . I Did it Again," for all the critics who called Brit a "one-hit wonder."

Brit and I in breathtaking Geneva, Switzerland. Brit did some recording; we both sneaked in a little sightseeing.

Britney and I stood with Shania Twain's horse at producer Mutt Lange's home in Geneva. I made this my Christmas card photo for 1999.

Brit with famous
photographer
Mark Selliger, who
designed the
Oops album cover.

Brit on an international
photo shoot. These
pictures are taken for
use in overseas teen
and music magazines.
Brit looked outrageous
in the hair extensions.

Britney with four of the hunky dancers, all in costume

And a really cool set

The video for the
title track on Britney's
second album, *Oops. . . I Did It Again*,
was filmed in March 2000. Once again,
legendary music video director Nigel Dick guided
the production. Here Brit and the dancers did
stretching and warm-up exercises.

*Fact
It's so fascinating and so fun to shoot a video. And the Oops...I Did It Again shoot was just amazing!

Britney in one of the "Oops" costumes. She wears three in the video.

The astronaut
"love interest"

Here's the space costume waiting for Britney.

*Fact:
When Britney is finished wearing a costume, it may be donated to the Rock 'n' Roll Hall of Fame or the Hard Rock Café to be exhibited, or given to a charity auction.*

Filming "Oops." During production on March 18, 2000, Brit was hit on the head by a piece of equipment and had to get four stitches.

Brit in her spacesuit about to be harnessed.

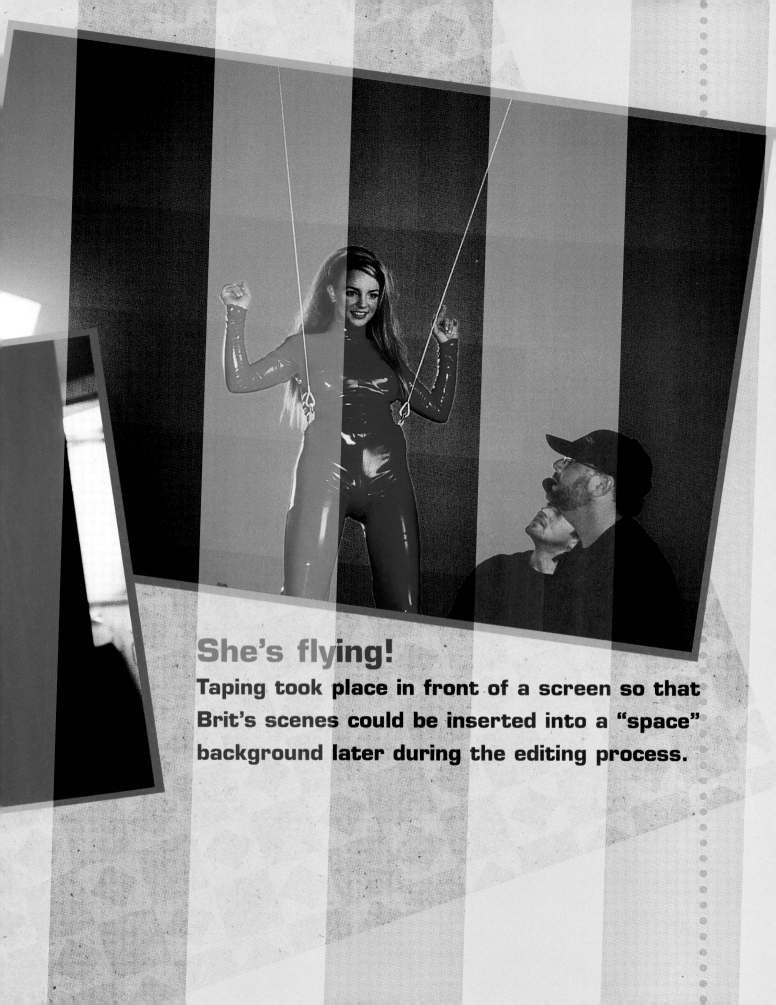

She's flying!

Taping took place in front of a screen so that Brit's scenes could be inserted into a "space" background later during the editing process.

Brit modeled
her shiny
"Star Trek"
hair.

She just loves my
coffee! Brit took a
break, but she has
to be careful not
to spoil her makeup
between takes.

Brit during a fitting for an *Oops* tour outfit. This is the silver jumpsuit; she also has one in solid gold.

One of the great things about Britney is her ability to have fun — anywhere, anyplace. No matter how grueling her schedule is, she's always laughing. Here she was in the limo with backup vocalists Kiley and Natalie.

Brit and I modeling hats with Karen White, wife of producer Eric Foster White. This picture was taken when Brit could still go shopping without being surrounded by fans. Sometimes she really misses the mall! And Karen.

A kiss for luck and she's on her way. Sending a Valentine's Day wish in February 1999.

We're talking
bad hair day!

Manuela,
who does Brit's hair
and makeup, working
her magic.

Brit and a few old friends acted up in Disney
World during summer 1999.

Brit with Mr. Mouse.
She'd just signed her name in cement
after a parade.

You can't take us anywhere! Brit and I goofed off at dinner in The Rainforest Café.

Britney — here with makeup artist Elan — looked like she needed a vacation. Actually, Brit loves to crack everybody up with her "faces."

Brit and sister Jamie Lynn caught some rays with MTV host Aranda in the Bahamas.

*Fact:
Big Rob our bodyguard is like our big brother. He takes such good care of us. His hometown is Alexandria, Virginia, so he's from the South just like Brit and me. He works out every day and can bench-press 380!

Car and Truck Rental

Brit and I took a spin around Disney World in this cool convertible. Big Rob directed people out of our way.

Britney's schedule has been nonstop all year. Here she is trying on costumes.

**Brit sending an
e-mail on her pager.**

Brit and I crowded together with 'N Sync's Lance Bass and Justin Timberlake during a cover shoot for Entertainment Weekly.

What's up, y'all?

Brit adores talking on the phone with her family and friends, and can pretty much find time anywhere to do it. Like in the car . . .

. . . in a hotel room . . .

. . . in her favorite ripped jeans and fuzzy slippers . . .

. . . on the bus . . .

. . . and even backstage during rehearsals. Here she's doing a "phoner" with a radio station.

Britney loves little dogs. Here's Mitzi, a Teacup Yorkshire terrier, one of our traveling companions who joined us at the Oribe salon. Brit had her color spruced up by Rita the magnificent in January 2000. . .

. . . while Mitzi got bored at the salon and tee-teed on the curtain.

The girls taking in the view before a party.

*Fact:
Mitzi weighs five
pounds, and eats
Eukenuba for
Puppies

Mitzi is such a star. We're going to get her some cool sunglasses too!

Mitzi enjoys riding in limos

*Fact: Bitzi weighs 3½ lbs., and loves to be carried around in her animal print bag.

This is Bitzi. She was supposed to be a gift for Brit's sister, Jamie Lynn, but Britney couldn't live without her. Who could resist that pretty face? Now she comes along with us too.

Baby joined Brit for a
video shoot in March 2000
while Mitzi was away
visiting the folks in
Louisiana for some much
needed obedience training.

Bitzi, or Baby,
as Brit calls her,
likes to have
her picture taken.

Brit catches a catnap with her puppy Bitzi standing guard.

Bitzi with her friend
Britney smile for the
camera.

Brit joined MTV for Spring Break in Cancun. The warm tropical breeze kept messing up her hair.

Baby Bitzi and Britney posed in Cancun.

Spring 2000, Britney made an appearance on Nickelodeon. There's the crowd from *All That*. Brit was nominated for two "Kids' Choice" Awards.

Nickelodeon!

Britney rehearsing for her "Crazy" tour on this awesome set

Lynne, Britney, and I all dressed up for the American Music Awards in 1998. Brit introduced the Goo Goo Dolls.

Back to the
American Music
Awards, this time
in January 2000.
Here I am posing
with the **Best New
Artist** winner, who
caused quite a
sensation in this
revealing jumpsuit.
Britney was so
excited to wear
this outfit by hot
designer Chloe
(Paul McCartney's
daughter).

At *Teen People*'s Anniversary Party, January 2000.

Brit models a costume candidate for the "Born to Make You Happy" video. That one went into the reject pile.

Backstage before a spring 2000 appearance. Brit's showing off her sassy new short hair.

Brit posed for a
People magazine cover,
January 2000,
on Malibu Beach.

One of Britney's fashion discoveries: airline slippers.

In March, Britney posed for MTV's "TRL Grammy Class of 2000" poster with other TRL alumni — like Jennifer Lopez, Limp Bizkit, Destiny's Child, and 'N Sync — for famed photographer David LaChapelle.

*Fact:
Brit thought she looked
like Lenny Kravitz. Then when
she got to the shoot, she
was seated right next
to him. Fun!

A *USA Weekend* photo shoot in January 2000

Grammy Awards
2000

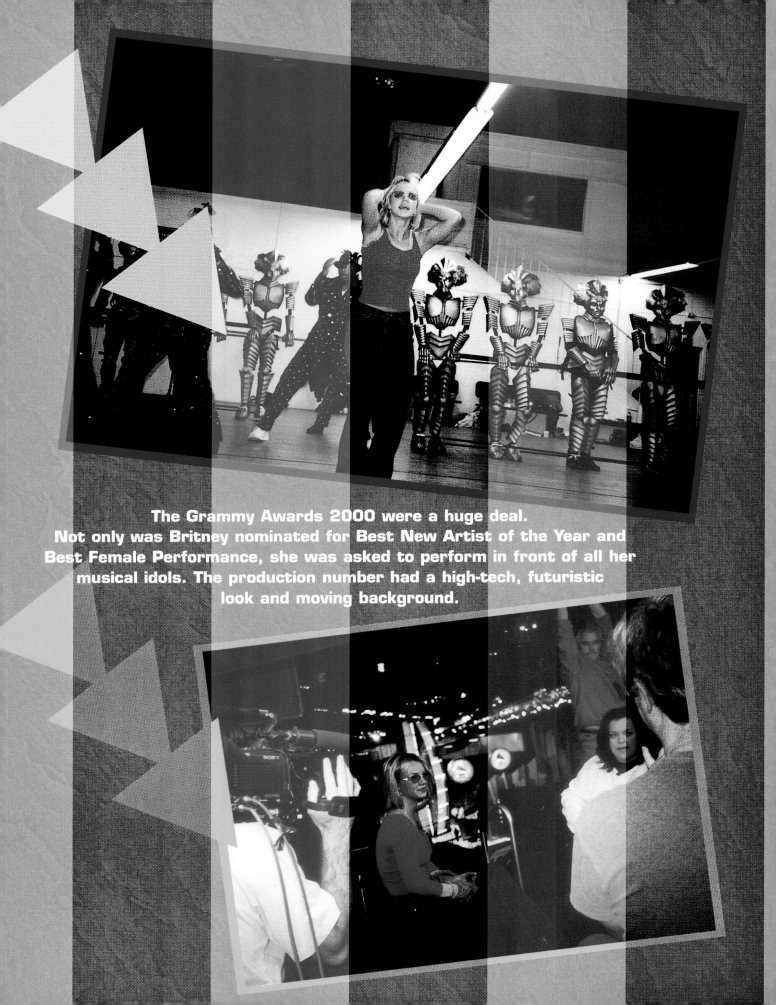

The Grammy Awards 2000 were a huge deal.
Not only was Britney nominated for Best New Artist of the Year and
Best Female Performance, she was asked to perform in front of all her
musical idols. The production number had a high-tech, futuristic
look and moving background.

Girlfriend Rosie O'Donnell stops to chat at the Grammy pre-show.

Grammy,
Grammy,
what shall
I wear?

In costume for the Grammy Awards 2000 performance of "From the Bottom of My Broken Heart." The demure beaded turtleneck top and tulle skirt, designed by Michael Bush, surprised critics.

*Fact:
Michael Bush designed many of Michael Jackson's tour costumes, including the glove and red jacket.

Grammy 2000 was the biggest night of Brit's career.
She needed the perfect look. Hair, nails, makeup,
designer jewelry. . .

. . . and a fabulous
Randolph Duke gown.
Amazing!

Ready to go!

Brit was decked out to meet the biggest names in the music industry at the Clive Davis party.

March 23, 2000.
Brit and I in Los Angeles poised to enter the Staples Center auditorium for the Grammy Awards 2000. We've come a long way since that fateful September in 1997.

Britney has become an international pop sensation!

I can't wait to see how far she'll go . . . and I'll be with her every step of the way.